MASTERING
THE SCRIPTURES

A Self-Study Course
In Effective Bible Study

by

Dr. James M. Cecy

JARON
MINISTRIES
INTERNATIONAL

Scripture quotations, unless otherwise noted, are taken from the New American Standard Bible, © 1960, 1962, 1963, 1968, 1971, 1972, 1973, 1975, 1977, 1995 by the Lockman Foundation. Used by permission.

Cover photo is the property of JARON Ministries International, Inc.

For further information about media and live seminars, contact:

JARON
MINISTRIES
INTERNATIONAL

4710 N Maple Ave, Fresno CA 93726

(559) 227-7997

email: office@jaron.org

JARON Ministries website: www.jaron.org

Dr. Cecy's website: www.puritywar.com

Campus Bible Church website: www.campusbiblechurch.com

Published by JARON Ministries International, Inc.

Printed in the USA.

ANCIENT WORDS

Verse 1

Holy words long preserved
For our walk in this world.
They resound with God's own heart
Oh, let the ancient words impart.
Words of life, words of hope
Give us strength, help us cope,
In this world, where e'er we roam
Ancient words will guide us home.

Chorus:

Ancient words ever true
Changing me and changing you.
We have come with open hearts
Oh, let the ancient words impart.

Verse 2

Holy words of our faith
Handed down to this age.
Came to us through sacrifice
Oh, heed the faithful words of Christ.
Holy words long preserved
For our walk in this world.
They resound with God's own heart
Oh, let the ancient words impart.

[Repeat Chorus]

Verse 3

Martyr's blood stains each page
They have died for this faith.
Hear them cry through the years
Heed these words and hold them dear.

[Repeat Chorus]

A WORD FROM THE AUTHOR

When I became a born-again believer in 1971, I had a voracious appetite to be well-versed in the Scriptures—from Genesis to Revelation. I began reading my Bible, sometimes three or four hours a day. I could not get enough. However, the more I read the more I knew I needed help. I was confused by some of the texts and misunderstood many others. Yet I had enough confidence in God to know the problem was not Him but me.

I took to heart the words of the apostle Paul in 2 Timothy 2:15, "Be diligent to present yourself approved to God as a workman who does not need to be ashamed, accurately handling the word of truth." I was also encouraged by the words of King Solomon in Ecclesiastes 12:11, "The words of wise men are like goads, and masters of these collections are like well-driven nails; they are given by one Shepherd."

I set out on the adventure of a lifetime—seeking daily to do the hard work of mastering the Scriptures, handling accurately the Word of God. I sought counsel from Bible teachers I trusted and bought Bible study tools I still use, even after forty-five years. I finished college, attended seminary and eventually completed a doctorate. However, after all that "book learning", I saw the need to simplify the process for myself and others. This workbook, that has gone through a series of changes, is the product of that continued quest.

I can assure you that after four decades of studying, preaching and teaching the Word of God, this method for effective Bible study, though not easy, will result in a depth of biblical understanding few take the effort to attain.

My prayer is that you will find this course of study more than just a useful tool. I trust it will help you become a well-driven nail, securely fastened to the One Shepherd who, in Scripture, clearly revealed Himself and taught us how we might live abundant lives (cf. John 10:10).

To God be the glory!

Dr. Jim Cecy

TABLE OF CONTENTS

Part Four: Designated Principles for Effective Bible Study

INTRODUCTION

I was in the Chicago area, teaching a community-wide conference. During one of the sessions, a distraught woman approached me and asked, "Dr. Cecy, can you recommend a book for me? My life is falling apart." I handed her my Bible. She handed it back to me and said, "No, no, I mean a current book that can really address my problems." I handed her my Bible. At this point she was insistent, "Can't you recommend a book that will really help me—maybe one that you've written?" Do you know how hard it was to not take that dear woman's credit card and fund my ministry with the sale of a pile of my materials? However, she did not need my books. She needed the Only Book—the Book of Books—the Word of God—the Holy Scriptures—the Sword of the Spirit—the Hammer of Justice—the Word of Truth—the Lamp unto our Feet—the Light unto our Path—the Word of Life. She needed the Bible—every one of those 66 life-changing books, 1,189 character-building chapters, 31,173 Spirit-led verses, and some 800,000 God-breathed words (depending on which version). She needed that marvelous love letter from God to man, written in three languages (Hebrew, Aramaic and Greek) by forty different authors (shepherds, judges, priests, kings, prophets, tax-collectors, physicians, etc.) from three different continents (Asia, Africa, Europe) over a period of 1600 years. And God wanted her—as He wants every one of us—to become masters of all it contains!

From the lips of the wise King Solomon we are told:

> "The words of wise men are like goads, and masters of these collections are like well-driven nails, they are given by one Shepherd" (Ecclesiastes 12:11).

And from the pen of the great apostle Paul we are challenged:

> "Be diligent to present yourself approved to God as a workman who does not need to be ashamed, handling accurately the word of truth" (2 Timothy 2:15).

Why go to all this trouble to master the Scriptures?

Because it's good for all of us!

"All Scripture is inspired by God and profitable for teaching, for reproof, for correction, for training in righteousness, that the man of God may be adequate, equipped for every good work" (2 Timothy 3:16-17).

"For the word of God is living and active and sharper than any two-edged sword, and piercing as far as the division of soul and spirit, of both joints and marrow, and able to judge the thoughts and intentions of the heart. And there is no creature hidden from His sight, but all things are open and laid bare to the eyes of Him with whom we have to do" (Hebrews 4:12-13).

It's even good for children of all ages:

" . . . from childhood (The Greek word *brephos* means *infancy*) you have known the sacred writings which are able to give you the wisdom that leads to salvation through faith which is in Christ Jesus" (2 Timothy 3:15).

Prayerfully complete the following:

I, _____, do sincerely agree to make every effort to complete this course in order to develop more effective personal Bible study habits.

If you have sincerely made that commitment, you join the ranks of such men of biblical fame as David, Ezra and Paul, and such men of church history as Wycliffe, Luther and Calvin. You also join the ranks of many of the greats of modern history who valued the Scriptures and saw them relevant for the times in which they lived—people such as:

1. Abraham Lincoln

"I believe the Bible is the best gift God has ever given to men. All the good from the Savior of the world is communicated to us through this book."

2. General Douglas MacArthur

"Believe me, sir, never a night goes by, be I ever so tired, but I read the Word of God before I go to bed."

3. William McKinley

"The more profoundly we study this wonderful Book, and the more closely we observe its divine precepts, the better citizens we will become and the higher will be our destiny as a nation."

4. Theodore Roosevelt

"A thorough knowledge of the Bible is worth more than a college education."

5. Dwight D. Eisenhower

"The Bible is endorsed by the ages. Our civilization is built upon its words. In no other book is there such a collection of inspired wisdom, reality and hope."

6. Herbert Hoover

"The study of this Book in your Bible classes is a post-graduate course in the richest library of human experience."

7. Andrew Jackson

"That book, sir, is the rock on which our republic stands."

8. George Washington

"It is impossible to rightly govern the world without God and the Bible."

9. Sir Walter Scott

"The most learned, acute and diligent student cannot, in the longest life, obtain an entire knowledge of this one volume. The more deeply he works the mine, the richer and more abundant he finds the ore; new light continually beams from this source of heavenly knowledge, to direct the conduct and illustrate the work of God and the ways of men; and he will at last leave the world confessing that the more he studied the Scriptures, the fuller conviction he had of his own ignorance, and of their inestimable value."

10. Woodrow Wilson

"The Bible is the Word of Life. I beg that you will read it and find this out for yourselves. Read, not little snatches here and there, but long passages that will be the road to the heart of it."

"I have a very simple thing to ask of you. I ask every man and woman in this audience that from this day on they will realize that part of the destiny of America lies in their daily perusal of this great Book."

"A man has deprived himself of the best there is in the world who has deprived himself of this (a knowledge of the Bible) . . . There are a good many problems before the American people today, and before me as President, but I expect to find the solution of those problems just in proportion that I am faithful in the study of the Word of God."

11. *Daniel Webster*

"If there is anything in my thoughts or style to commend, the credit is due to my parents for instilling in me an early love of the Scriptures. If we abide by the principles taught in the Bible, our county will go on prospering and to prosper; but if we and our posterity neglect its instructions and authority, no man can tell how sudden a catastrophe may overwhelm us and bury all our glory in profound obscurity."

12. *Alfred Lord Tennysen*

"Bible reading is an education in itself."

How About Us?

If the history books of the future were to record our present commitment to the Word of God, what might they say?

_____

_____

_____

1. *The Goal of Effective Bible Study*

I would not even want to try to log the number of miles I have traveled, teaching the Word of God in hundreds of churches, schools and conference centers on five continents. I have sat under coconut trees in Asia and in great cathedrals in Europe. I am quick to remind folks that the longest journey in the world is not around the world but from our heads to our hearts.

However, the first step in the journey to becoming an effective Bible student is not learning language arts or linguistic techniques. It is not buying a pile of those "other" books. It begins with the basics— understanding the ultimate goal—to have the Word of God "abide" in us (cf. 1 John 2:14).

> **The goal of effective Bible study is getting**
>
> **the mind of God into the attitudes and actions of men.**

This is not an easy task. In order for us to know the mind of God, God had to communicate with us. God Himself spoke of the difficulty with which finite men would struggle to understand His infinite mind.

"'For my thoughts are not your thoughts, neither are your ways my ways,' declares the Lord. 'for as the heavens are higher than the earth, so are My ways higher than your ways, and My thoughts than your thoughts'" (Isaiah 55:8-9).

And again in the New Testament:

"Oh, the depths of the riches both of the wisdom and knowledge of God! How unsearchable are His judgments and unfathomable His ways! For who has known the mind of the Lord, or who became His counselor?" (Romans 11:33-34).

As difficult as it is for man to understand the mind of the Lord, God Himself made it possible for us to understand it, at least in part.

Moses encouraged the sons of Israel with these words:

"The secret things belong to the Lord our God, but the things revealed belong to us and our sons forever . . ." (Deuteronomy 29:29).

Through the Prophet Isaiah, the Lord gave this added encouragement:

"For as the rain and the snow come down from heaven, and do not return there without watering the earth, and making it bear and sprout, and furnishing seed to the sower and bread to the eater; so shall My word be which goes forth from My mouth; it shall not return to Me empty, without accomplishing what I desire, and without succeeding in the matter for which I sent it" (Isaiah 55:10-11).

This brings us to two very important questions:

QUESTION #1

How has the mind of God been revealed to us?

QUESTION #2

How do we get the mind of God into the attitudes and actions of men?

The answer is the same for both. It all happens through:

Revelation → the process by which God spoke His mind to men.

Inspiration → the method by which God Himself spoke through human authors His exact revelation to men.

Transmission → the miraculous and sacrificial preservation of the Scriptures throughout human history.

Translation → the careful translation of the original language manuscripts of Scripture into various languages.

Interpretation → the accurate understanding of the meaning of Scripture in light of its historical, grammatical context.

Illumination → the ministry of the Holy Spirit in the life of the believer to produce the proper response to Scripture.

Application → the careful attempt at demonstrating the Scripture's relevancy in human lives so that a change in attitudes and actions occurs.

---

2. The Method of Effective Bible Study

Bible study method books abound. Some are simple; some exhaustive. Those that are most reliable are those that utilize what is called *historical, grammatical exegesis.* What does all this mean?

1. *Historical.* Scripture was not written in an historical vacuum. We study every portion of Scripture in light of its historical and cultural context.

2. *Grammatical.* God chose the vehicle of three human languages to communicate His Word to us: Hebrew and Aramaic for the Old Testament and Koine (common) Greek for the New Testament. When God spoke; He spoke well. Using the grammatical method we interpret Scripture in light of the nuances of the words and grammar in the text.

3. *Exegesis.* This word comes from a Greek word meaning "to lead out" and speaks of pulling truths out of Scripture (exegesis) rather than reading opinions into Scripture (eisegesis). It is critical that we primarily draw our biblical conclusions from the facts of Scripture (inductive study), rather than having already formulated conclusions and attempting to find facts in the Bible to support those conclusions (deductive study).

We believe in . . .

Verbal Plenary Inspiration

Verbal → Every word found in the Bible is given by God.

Plenary → Everything in the Bible is authoritative.

Inspiration → Everything in the Bible is divinely directed.

---

3. The Process of Effective Bible Study

The process of effective Bible study is called *hermeneutics*.

This word is taken from the Greek word *hermeneuo* which means to interpret or explain. In particular, hermeneutics is the process of explaining the single meaning of Scripture. As one of my seminary professors so aptly said, *"Hermeneutics teaches us how to know what the Bible means by what it says."* Rather than pursuing what the text means to us, we are to search out what God Himself intended to say.

This was the process Ezra used to teach the people of Israel:

> "And they read from the book, from the law of God, translating (lit. explaining, using hermeneutics) to give the sense so that they understood the reading" (Nehemiah 8:8).

And it was this same process of hermeneutics that Jesus used to explain Scripture to the men on the road to Emmaus.

> "And beginning with Moses and with all the prophets, He explained to them the things concerning Himself in all the Scriptures . . . . Then He opened their minds to understand the Scriptures" (Luke 24:27, 45).

Let's Review:

#1 The goal of effective Bible Study is getting the mind of God into the attitudes and actions of men.

#2 The method of effective Bible Study is called historical, grammatical exegesis.

#3 The process of effective Bible Study is called hermeneutics.

PART ONE
DOCTRINAL PRESUPPOSITIONS FOR EFFECTIVE BIBLE STUDY

Before we learn how to study the Bible we must understand some fundamental doctrine:

1. Concerning God and His Word

#1. God spoke . . . .

"So shall My word be which goes forth from My mouth . . . " (Isaiah 55:11).

" . . . Thy word is truth" (John 17:17).

"Thus saith the Lord . . . " or "The Word of the LORD came unto me . . . " (e.g. Isaiah 44:6 and 2,600 other times)

Sometimes the Scriptures are even called *oracles* (i.e. inspired utterances) (cf. Proverbs 30:1; 31:1; Isaiah 13:1; Jeremiah 23:33; Acts 7:38; etc.)

#2. God spoke through men . . .

"But know this, first of all, that no prophecy of Scripture is a matter of one's own interpretation, for no prophecy was ever made by an act of human will, but men moved by the Holy Spirit spoke from God" (2 Peter 1:20-21).

"And for this reason we also constantly thank God that when you received from us the word of God's message, you accepted it not as the word of men, but for what it really is, the word of God, which also performs its work in you who believe" (1 Thessalonians. 2:13).

"And when they heard this, they lifted their voices to God with one accord and said, 'O Lord, it is Thou . . . who by the Holy Spirit, through the mouth of our father David Thy servant, didst say . . . '" (Acts 4:24-25; cf. Acts 1:16).

#3. *God spoke through men that which is both reliable and profitable.*

"Thy word I have treasured in my heart, that I might not sin against Thee" (Psalm 119:11).

"Thy word has revived me" (Psalm 119:50b).

"Thy word is very pure, therefore Thy servant loves it" (Psalm 119:140).

"Where there is no vision (i.e. divine revelation/hearing from God), the people are unrestrained (i.e. naked and exposed) . . . " (Proverbs 30:18).

"Every word of God is tested; He is a shield to those who take refuge in Him. Do not add to His words lest He reprove you, and you be proved a liar" (Proverbs 30:5-6).

"For truly I say to you, until heaven and earth pass away, not the smallest letter or stroke shall pass away from the Law, until all is accomplished" (Matthew 5:18).

" . . . I did not shrink from declaring to you anything that was profitable . . . " (Acts 20:20).

" . . . from childhood you have known the sacred writings which are able to give you the wisdom that leads to salvation through faith which is in Christ Jesus. All Scripture is inspired by God and profitable for teaching, for reproof, for correction, for training in righteousness; that the man of God may be adequate, equipped for every good work" (2 Timothy 3:15-17).

" . . . building yourselves up on your most holy faith . . . " (Jude 1:20).

One theologian has put it all together with this helpful definition of inspiration:

> *"Inspiration is God's superintending of human authors so that, using their own individual personalities, they composed and recorded without error in the original autographs His revelation to man."* (Charles C. Ryrie, The Ryrie Study Bible, Moody Press, 1978, p. 1983)

2. Concerning Us and God's Word

When it comes to effective Bible study, there are three important rules to follow:

Rule #1 The Bible is to be read thoroughly.

We need to develop a habit of regular Bible reading in order to familiarize ourselves with all the content of Scripture. From the wealth of our personal reflection and general overview of the Word of God we will be able to much more effectively interpret specific passages.

See Appendix 6 for a Bible Reading Record in which you can keep track of your regular Bible reading.

> Bible reading is truly a treasure hunt!

The more we dig; the more we find. Take a moment and read Job 28 and write down your observations concerning the value of digging into Scripture:

_____

_____

_____

Rule #2 - The Bible is to be interpreted literally.

Scripture is not written in some secret, spiritual code or in some mysterious, ethereal way. When God communicated, He communicated clearly and in a way that His children could understand. Therefore, Scripture can be taken to mean exactly what it says. Follow this simple guideline: "When the plain sense makes sense, make no other sense."

We call this: **Plain Literal Interpretation**

However, let me hasten to say that Scripture should be taken to mean exactly what it says unless the context or the expression itself indicates otherwise.

For example, in Matthew 23:14, Jesus says, "Woe to you, scribes and Pharisees, hypocrites, because you devour widow's houses . . . " No one in their right mind would suggest that these men were literally eating the houses of these widows. And when the Bible speaks of the "four corners of the earth" none of us need panic over the scientific inaccuracy of this figure of speech, just as we would not react to the mention in the Bible of the sun setting, when we know that it really is the earth rotating! The Bible is filled with figurative language and should be interpreted accordingly.

This we call: **Figurative Literal Interpretation**

Rule #3 - The Bible is to be studied diligently.

There are no shortcuts to being an effective Bible student.

> "Be diligent to present yourself approved to God as a workman who does not need to be ashamed, handling accurately the word of truth" (2 Timothy 2:15; cf. 2 Peter 3:16).

The Psalms speak of the successful, prosperous believer whose delight is in the law of the Lord and in His law he meditates day and night (cf. Psalm 1:2-3) .

The apostle Peter spoke of some of the apostle Paul's epistles being "hard to understand, which the untaught and unstable distort, as they do also the rest of Scriptures, to their own destruction" (2 Peter 2:16).

Rule #4 - The Bible is to be applied generously.

Although there is only one interpretation of Scripture, there are many applications.

> "All Scripture is inspired by God and profitable . . . for teaching, for reproof, for correction, for training in righteousness" (2 Timothy 3:16).

Even studying the things that happened to the people of God thousands of years before Christ has tremendous application to us today. Read 1 Corinthians 10:1-14. What is the major point of this passage? _____

_____

The writer of the letter to the Hebrews addressed how deeply the Word of God penetrates our lives:

"For the word of God is living and active and sharper than any two-edged sword, and piercing as far as division of soul and spirit, of both joints and marrow, and able to judge the thoughts and intentions of the heart" (Hebrews 4:12).

"For the overseer must be above reproach as God's steward . . . holding fast the faithful word which is in accordance with the teaching, so that he will be able both to exhort in sound doctrine and to refute those who contradict" (Titus 1:7-9).

A Personal Lesson from Psalm 19:7-14

Read carefully through the detailed outline of Psalm 19:7-14 in Appendix 5 entitled "God Has Spoken in His Marvelous Word."

1. Write out the six key words that are presented as **facets** of the Word of God.

   a _____ b. _____ c. _____

   d. _____ e. _____ f. _____

2. Write out the six key words that are presented as **characteristics** of the Word of God.

   a _____ b. _____ c. _____

   d. _____ e. _____ f. _____

3. Write out the six key phrases that are presented as the **ways** God's Word impacts out lives.

   a. _____

   b. _____

   c. _____

   d. _____

   e. _____

   f. _____

4. Write out David's four **testimonies** reflecting his attraction to the Word of God.

   a _____

   b. _____

   c. _____

   d. _____

Let's Review:

I. Concerning God and His Word:

   1. God spoke . . . .

   2. God spoke through men . . . .

   3. God spoke through men that which is both reliable and profitable.

II. Concerning us and God's Word:

   1. The Bible is to be read thoroughly

   2. The Bible is to be interpreted literally.

   3. The Bible is to be studied diligently.

PART TWO
DIVINE PREREQUISITES FOR EFFECTIVE BIBLE STUDY

Before we can learn to effectively interpret and apply Scripture, there must be certain conditions that exist in our lives.

Prerequisite #1 - A Regenerate Heart

The story is told of a college professor who stood before his class and exclaimed, "I've read the Bible and it didn't make a bit of sense to me. I'm still an atheist." A Christian in the room stood and said, "Sir, I can explain why you were not able to understand the Bible. I believe that the Bible is God's love letter to His children. That's what you get for reading somebody else's mail!"

I need the constant reminder that the Bible is more than a textbook; it is a personal correspondence from God to His children—those who have trusted in the Crucified and Risen Lord Jesus Christ alone for their salvation (cf. John 1:12). As such we have been given the ability, because of His indwelling Holy Spirit, to understand the content and implications of the Scriptures we read. So said the apostle Paul:

> " . . . the thoughts of God no one knows except the Spirit of God. Now we (i.e. believers) have received, not the spirit of the world, but the Spirit who is from God, that we might know the things freely given to us by God . . . . But a natural man (i.e. an unbeliever) does not accept the things of the Spirit of God, for they are foolishness to him and he cannot understand them, because they are spiritually appraised" (1 Corinthians 2:11-12, 14).

A regenerate heart is absolutely essential to effective Bible study. This is not to say that an unbeliever cannot understand the content of Scripture. He too, can follow the basic rules of Bible interpretation (hermeneutics). However, because of his heart of unbelief he will resist application of those Scriptures that bring correction or judgment to his sinful condition. His conclusions will be filtered through his unbelieving, unregenerate nature (cf. 2 Peter 2:16). For example, he may conclude that the Bible teaches that Jesus was the Risen Christ and at the same time deny the Risen Lord's power to change him.

"Is this not the reason you are mistaken, that you do not understand the Scriptures, or the power of God?" (Mark 12:24)

Take a moment and write out your personal testimony concerning your decision to trust in Jesus Christ alone for your salvation.

_____

_____

_____

_____

_____

_____

_____

_____

_____

In the front of every new Bible (and I do have many) I write the words:

Dear Jim,

On the back page I write:

Love,

God, Your Heavenly Father

If you haven't already done so, why not do the same in your Bible?

Prerequisite #2 - A Receptive Life

In his epistle, James, the brother of our Lord, writes concerning some of the prerequisites for responding properly to the word of truth. Specifically, in James 1:19-27, he lists out the qualities that I believe must be found in the life of all believers who wish to get the most out of their time studying the Word of God.

Take a moment to evaluate yourself in light of these (Circle your score):

1. An Open Ear - "Be quick to hear" (James 1:19).

Winning	Struggling	Losing
10 9 8	7 6 5 4	3 2 1

2. A Cautious Tongue - "slow to speak" (James 1:19).

Winning	Struggling	Losing
10 9 8	7 6 5 4	3 2 1

3. A Calm Head - "slow to anger" (James 1:19-20).

Winning	Struggling	Losing
10 9 8	7 6 5 4	3 2 1

4. A Pure Life - "putting aside filthiness . . . and wickedness" (James 1:21).

Winning	Struggling	Losing
10 9 8	7 6 5 4	3 2 1

5. A Teachable Spirit - "in humility receive the word" (James 1:21).

Winning	Struggling	Losing
10 9 8	7 6 5 4	3 2 1

6. An Obedient Heart - "prove yourself doers of the word" (James 1:22-24).

Winning	Struggling	Losing
10 9 8	7 6 5 4	3 2 1

7. A Searching Mind - "looks intently at the perfect law" (James 1:25).

Winning	Struggling	Losing
10 9 8	7 6 5 4	3 2 1

8. A Controlled Tongue - "bridle his tongue" (James 1:26).

Winning	Struggling	Losing
10 9 8	7 6 5 4	3 2 1

9. A Merciful Hand - "visit widows and orphans in their distress" (James 1:27).

Winning	Struggling	Losing
10 9 8	7 6 5 4	3 2 1

10. A Separated Body - "keep oneself unstained by the world" (James 1:27).

Winning	Struggling	Losing
10 9 8	7 6 5 4	3 2 1

Which of the above areas need the most work? _____

"The Bible will keep you from sin or sin will keep you from the Bible."
(D.L. Moody)

Prerequisite #3 - A Clear-Thinking Mind

Perhaps you are familiar with Socrates, the Athenian philosopher who lived four centuries before Christ. One day a young man came to him saying, "I want knowledge." Socrates took the boy into the river and pushed his head under water until bubbles came to the surface. The teacher then asked the student, "What did you want most?" Gasping, the young man answered, "I wanted air! I wanted air!" Socrates replied, "When you want knowledge as much as you just wanted air, you will find it."

Effective Bible study (hermeneutics) takes brain-work—lots of it! Bible study may be a spiritual adventure but it does not mean the Holy Spirit bypasses our mind. It is time to clean out the cob-webs and start polishing those brain-cells. Hermeneutics is a literary science, using much the same rules for interpreting sacred Scripture as interpreting secular literature, like Shakespeare. The most effective Bible students are those who also have a general knowledge of history, science, geography, and language, especially grammar. So, pull out those old textbooks. We are going to need them.

In addition to polishing up our general knowledge, it is also valuable to begin (or continue) a regular program of Scripture memorization—especially meditating on those passages that relate to the value of Scripture (e.g. Joshua 1:8; Psalm 1:1-3; Psalm 19:7-9; Psalm 119:9-11; Ecclesiastes 12:11-12; John 17:17; 2 Timothy 3:16 and Hebrews 4:12).

Of course, if we do not yet have the names of the books of both the Old and New Testaments memorized, we best get on with it right away— "Genesis, Exodus, Leviticus, Numbers, Deuteronomy . . . Matthew, Mark, Luke, John . . . " The days when we have to run to the lists of books in the front of our Bibles need to be over!

Let's Review:

If we are going to be effective Bible students we must have:

1. A regenerate heart

2. A receptive life

3. A clear-thinking mind

PART THREE
DOCTRINAL PUBLICATIONS FOR EFFECTIVE BIBLE STUDY

I am committed to the fact that there are only two categories of books—*The Holy Bible* and *Everything Else*. Only the Word of God is inspired and completely trustworthy as the source of our faith and practice (2 Timothy 3:16).

Having presented many of the Scriptures themselves on how to study the Bible itself, I am now taking the risk of suggesting we gather resources outside of the Bible—i.e. the *other* books. My first concern is that my short list of specific tools excludes many other helpful resources, old and new and yet to come. That is why I chose to merely present the categories of Bible study tools.

Secondly, I fear that my recommendation implies an endorsement of everything these materials might present. I encourage you to be a discerning reader, like the Bereans in Paul's day, examining the Scriptures to see if what you are reading (or hearing) is biblically sound and comes from a reliable source (cf. Acts 17:11).

Suggested Bible Study Tools

Wise King Solomon said it well,

> "But beyond this, my son, be warned: the writing of many books is endless, and excessive devotion to books is wearying to the body". (Ecclesiastes 12:12).

Just one view of a Christian bookstore and one gets the feeling Solomon hit the nail on the head.

And yet, as serious Bible students, purchasing the right biblical and secular resources can save us much time and effort . . . and even money. Excessive devotion to books is not only wearying to the body; it is also wearying to the pocketbook!

Below is a list of categories of basic tools I believe will be useful for effective Bible study. Many of the resources are available in print and electronically.

Every Bible student should own (or have easy access to) at least:

1. Two Whole Bible Translations

Find translations of the Bible that attempt to stay as close to the original Hebrew and Greek texts as possible and still be understandable.

2. One Bible Paraphrase

These works, though not literal word-for-word translations, help to expand our understanding of the text.

3. One Complete Bible Concordance

A concordance presents alphabetically every occurrence of every word in the Bible. Most present the Hebrew, Aramaic and Greek words.

4. One Bible Encyclopedia or Dictionary

These references define specific biblical terms, people and places as well as related topics, such as archaeology and culture.

5. One Dictionary of New Testament and Old Testament Words

These works (sometimes called lexicons) explain the meanings of the New Testament Greek words or the Old Testament Hebrew/Aramaic words in their biblical and historical context.

6. One Bible Handbook (Survey of Old and New Testament)

These mini-commentaries also present the historical and archaeological background to each of the books of the Bible, as well as a brief outline and explanation of each chapter.

7. One Systematic Theology (Bible Doctrine)

These books present an organized treatment of the major doctrines regarding Scripture, God, man, sin, salvation, Christ, the Holy Spirit, Satan, angels, heaven, hell, the church, etc.

8. One Commentary of the Whole Bible

These commentaries briefly explain every major portion of Scripture. We may also want to look for single-volume commentaries of either the Old Testament or New Testament.

9. Commentaries on Specific Books of the Bible

If possible, look for a commentary written or produced by a Bible teacher or Christian publisher you respect.

Before looking for an individual commentary, study a particular passage as thoroughly as you are able (following the steps in this manual) and then examine the commentary to see if the author deals carefully with the same text. Is it truly a helpful resource for you?

10. Other Helpful Biblical Resources

- A topical Bible, organizing by subject
- An inter-linear Bible, presenting side-by-side versions of the text
- A Bible atlas containing maps and charts (Note: Some are found in the back of many Bibles)
- A guide to parallel passages (e.g. A harmony of the Gospels)
- A single volume dictionary or textbook on church history

11. Secular Helps

- An exhaustive dictionary in the same language as your Bible version
- A grammar textbook in the same language as your Bible version.
- A general knowledge encyclopedia
- A thesaurus that lists words in groups of synonyms and antonyms
- A book of quotes and illustrations
- A brief history and timeline of ancient history

Note: Many people choose to purchase a Study Bible available in their favorite translations or paraphrases that has a limited amount of some of these tools.

Evaluating Your Personal Library

List what resources you presently have (or have easy access to) and what you need for your personal library:

---

1. Bible Translations:

    I have:

    I need:

---

2. Bible Paraphrases:

    I have:

    I need:

---

3. Bible Concordance:

    I have:

    I need:

4. Bible Encyclopedia or Dictionary:

I have:

I need:

5. Dictionary of New and Old Testament Words:

I have:

I need:

6. Bible Handbook (Survey of Old and New Testament):

I have:

I need:

7. Systematic Theology (Bible Doctrine):

I have:

I need:

8. Commentary of the Whole Bible (or Old or New Testament):

I have:

I need:

9. Commentaries on Specific Books of the Bible:

I have:

I need:

10. Other Biblical Resources:

I have:

I need:

11. Secular Helps:

I have:

I need:

PART FOUR
DESIGNATED PRINCIPLES FOR EFFECTIVE BIBLE STUDY

I love the very old story of the woman trying to impress the new pastor who was visiting her home for the first time. During their conversation she spoke to her young daughter, "Go get the book that Mommy loves best." The little girl brought back the Sears Catalog! (Does anybody remember those? Perhaps today she would have brought her mother's laptop, open to Amazon or eBay.)

Let's be honest. Like this mother, if the truth be told, many of us are just as susceptible to sporadic Bible reading and even less in-depth study. Even the most devout among us suffer great lapses in attempting to engage in effective Bible study, simply because we think we do not know how. We marvel at gifted Bible teachers. We wonder where they get all that insight.

Although, it is true that God does bestow special insight as He wills to do so, it is also true that He will illumine the Scriptures for all who will work hard to "handle accurately the word of truth" (2 Timothy 2:15).

With that in mind, we come now to a simple but very effective five step Bible study procedure, each which is to be done in this order:

P.O.I.A.P.

Step One: Preparation: Anticipating God's Direction

Step Two: Observation: Asking The Right Questions

Step Three: Interpretation: Answering The Right Questions

Step Four: Application: Applying The Right Answers

Step Five: Presentation: Announcing The Good News

> To get the most out of the remainder of this workbook I encourage you to select a Bible text of no more than 2-3 verses to work through.
>
> My Text: _____

Step One
Preparation
Anticipating God's Direction

1. Begin With Prayer

It is vital to effective Bible study that we first spend time preparing our heart and mind to study God's Holy Word. I like to use a prayer reminder based on the model prayer given by Jesus in His Sermon on the Mount (cf. Matthew 6:9-13).

P.R.A.Y.E.R

P = Praising God for who He is and what He has done in my life

R = Repenting and asking God to forgive me of my sin

A = Asking God to use my time of study for His glory

Y = Yielding my will to His, in a spirit of humility and obedience

E = Entreating for others who will benefit from my study

R = Rejoicing in what God will accomplish even before it happens

2. Make a Commitment

Before we begin our study we need to think through the following statement and prayerfully sign it now and review it each time we approach the Scriptures:

"Believing that God has clearly revealed what I otherwise could not know, I will endeavor to apply these principles in order to find the single meaning of Scripture and, by God's power, creatively apply it."

_____

(My Signature)

---

3. Proceed with Caution

Remember that we are interested in inductive Bible study whereby we draw our conclusions from the facts of Scripture (exegesis). Beware of deductive Bible study whereby we approach Scripture with pre-conceived ideas as to what it says and then set out to force verses to prove it (eisegesis). Be careful not to make the Bible passage say what we want it to say. Constantly keep in mind that it is God's word and not ours (cf. 1 Thessalonians 2:13).

Step Two
Observation
Asking The Right Questions

1. Study the Background of the Book

Using various Bible Study Tools (listed in Part Three) go to Appendix 2 of this workbook and begin jotting notes in "How to Do a Survey of a Book of the Bible".

Continue by using those same tools to complete the worksheet in Appendix 3 entitled, "How to Do a Biblical Character Study".

On a separate piece of paper entitled "Background" write out the pertinent information concerning the author, date and place written, theme, geography and culture, etc.

Let's Practice . . .

2. Read the Entire Book and Chapter

Keeping in mind the background information on the book, it's now time to read through the entire book. Read the particular chapter a number of times (no less than three), using various translations and paraphrases. (Now do you see why a regular program of daily Bible reading is critical to effective Bible study?)

Take note of any specific connections the verse or verses being studied have with the rest of the book. Why is it written in that particular chapter, book, division (e.g. historical books, wisdom literature, prophets, Gospels, Epistles, etc.), and testament (old or new)? Keep in mind that "text without context is pretext."

Let's Practice . . .

---

3. Examine Carefully the Specific Passage

Again using numerous different translations and paraphrases, read the passage over at least a dozen times. Take note of the major differences in the various translations.

Look for the flow of the text, paying attention to such words as "Therefore" (drawing you to what was previously written), "If . . . then . . . " (pointing out cause and effect), contrasts and comparisons, repetitions in key words or ideas, etc.

Let's Practice . . .

---

4. Ask Appropriate Questions

Jot down a series of questions about the passage. Give no answers at this point.

Use the six questions you learned in grammar school: Who? What? Where? When? How? Why? Asking these questions of every word and phrase in the passage may, at first, seem tedious, especially since many of the questions are either absurd or obvious. However, this exercise will help unlock the Scriptures. The essence of biblical scholarship is first asking the right questions of the text in order to find the right answers. Identify the most important questions.

> **Let's Practice . . .**

5. Look Up Cross-References

Using the notes in the margin of some Bibles, your concordance or helpful reference works, take note of important cross-references. Write down how these cross-references might relate to the passage you are studying. Be very careful at this point. Cross-references are not inspired and may not, in reality, relate to the passage. When in doubt, don't use that particular cross-reference.

> **Let's Practice . . .**

6. Write Down Any Further Observations

Does the text carry from a previous verse or chapter? Does it flow into the text? For example, the first verse of Romans 8 is directly related to the last verse of Romans 7.

In some Bibles we will find words that are in *italics*. This is not for emphasis! Instead, it means that these words were not a part of the original text but were added by the translators for clarification. Any words or verses in [brackets] are considered questionable. Also note that the chapter and verse divisions were not a part of the original text. Refer to a detailed commentary for further help in these matters.

> **Let's Practice . . .**

Step Three
Interpretation
Answering The Right Questions

Our goal in this step is to find the answers to the most critical of the questions we asked in Step Two. This is the step where we once again use whatever resources are available to us.

1. Do Particular Word Studies

Using such helps as Bible dictionaries, concordances, word study helps and commentaries, attempt to write out a clear definition and explanation for every key word and phrase in the text. This may involve doing a brief history of the word or phrase (called an etymology). Be sure to pay particular attention to how the word or phrase was used in the day it was written—not before or after. What did it mean to them? Watch for synonyms (words that have similar meanings), antonyms (words that have opposite meanings), figures of speech (metaphors, similes, etc.), idioms, repeated words and phrases. Of course, a keen Bible student will also be aware of what words one might have expected but are not in the text.

Let's Practice . . .

---

2. Watch for Specific Details in the Grammar

Pay particular attention to conjunctions (but, and, etc.) and prepositions (in, by, around, upon, through, etc.) Again using the proper tools, examine each key verb as to the tense (past, present, future, etc.), voice (active, passive, middle), mood (indicative, subjunctive, etc.) and number (first, second or third person singular or plural). If we don't know what these terms mean, we will need to look them up in that old grammar book we dusted off. It will be well worth the effort. For example, the indicative mood tells us something is happening, the subjunctive mood suggests that something might happen and the imperative mood points us to what must happen. Those are important distinctions.

Let's Practice:

3. Write Down What Others Say About This Text

Let me hasten to say that this is never the first step. Write down only those things that are particular answers to those questions you feel are most important. (Now do you see why proper observation of the text is so important?)

Let's Practice:

4. Begin Problem Solving

Our job as "approved workman" (2 Timothy 2:15) is, to the best of our God-given ability, find that single meaning God intended. Obviously, not all of our commentaries and other resources are going to be in agreement on every detail of the text. Well-meaning scholars we trust may even agree to disagree. That's the beauty of having many teachers in the Body of Christ (cf. Ephesians 4:11-16). We must also learn to master the Scriptures ourselves so that we might be more effective in identifying those "wolves in sheep's clothing"—those deceptive Bible-abusers who bring ruin to our faith (cf. Matthew 7:15; 2 Peter 2:1-22; Jude 1:3-19).

As truth-seeking Bible students, we must carefully compare the different views and decide what seems to be the best interpretation. Just make sure you carefully support that view with Scripture. It's quite appropriate to say, "I'm not sure my view is correct but from the study I have done, let me tell you what I think God intended to say in this passage."

By the way, if the passage we are studying is a parable (e.g. Luke 5 -8,12-20) there is a helpful fill-in sheet in Appendix 4, entitled "Instructions For Interpreting Parables."

Ultimately, we must keep in mind the warnings not to add or subtract from Scripture:

> "You shall not add to the word which I am commanding you, nor take away from it . . ." (Deuteronomy 4:2).

> "Do not add to His words or He will reprove you, and you will be proved a liar" (Proverbs 30:6).

> " . . . if anyone takes away from the words of the book of this prophecy, God shall take away his part from the tree of life . . . " (Revelation 22:19).

Let's Practice:

Step Four
Application
Applying The Right Answers

Although there is only one interpretation of the passage we are studying, there may be many applications. At this point we have already answered the questions: Who? What? Where? When? How? and Why? The key question we need to answer in this step is: So what? In other words, we have observed the passage and asked the right questions. We have interpreted the passage and answered those questions. How are we going to get this passage to take effect in lives—ours and others?

Skipping this step makes our study merely academic.

"But prove yourself doers of the word, and not merely hearers who delude themselves" (James 1:22; cf. 2 Timothy 3:16).

"If I . . . know all knowledge . . . but do not have love, I am nothing" (1 Corinthians 13:2).

During this step we re-examine what we have studied and make a list of the:

- Commands to obey
- Promises to keep
- Truths to know
- Actions to take

- Sins to forsake
- Examples to follow
- Things to avoid
- New thoughts about God

Let's Practice:

We're not through yet! There is still another question that must be asked: Now what? We have learned steps one to four: preparation, observation, interpretation and application. Though these first four steps may seem overwhelming to the beginner, this next step is also vitally important.

Step Five
Presentation
Announcing The Good News

It has been well said that people don't care how much we know until they know how much we care. God never called us to study Scripture merely for our own edification but also for the edification of others. Effective Bible students care that what they have worked so hard to glean for themselves must also be effectively shared with others. Consider just a couple of the many Scriptures related to the importance of teaching what we learn:

> "And we proclaim Him, admonishing every man and teaching every man with all wisdom, that we may present every man complete in Christ . . . Let the word of Christ richly dwell within you, with all wisdom teaching and admonishing one another . . . "
> (Colossians 1:28; 3:16).

> " . . . let us consider how to stimulate one another to love and good deeds . . . encouraging one another; and all the more, as you see the day drawing near" (Hebrews 10:24-25).

At this point, we must decide what we want our listeners (or readers) to know, feel and do, given the time or the space allowed. Beyond the biblical content, is what we are about to teach practical, measureable and attainable?

1. Organize the Presentation

All the best research in the world is nothing without effective presentation. Although this course is primarily about *hermeneutics* (Bible study) and not *homiletics* (preaching), there are some basic principles that must be considered.

I like to design a message, using the analogy of an airplane flight. The introduction tells the listener where the message is going and strives to make the journey worthwhile, even exciting. The main points show specific progress along the way. The illustrations break up the trip with vista points that are of interest. The conclusion gives a soft landing and points to the open door—with the plane on time and where it promised it would be.

2. Select Appropriate Illustrations

Illustrations are the windows of a message. They can be drawn from:

- Bible stories ("Scripture illustrating Scripture")
- Personal testimonies
- Brief quotes and selected illustrations
- Carefully-chosen humor
- Graphics, pictures, maps and charts
- Nature
- Poetry or song lyrics
- Other stories and anecdotes
- Life observations

Let's Practice:

"Most people are bothered by those passages of scripture they do not understand, but the passages that bother me are those I do understand."

(Mark Twain)

SAMPLE PERSONAL ILLUSTRATION

"My Encounter With Colossians 3"

One night I experienced a horrible graphic dream that is much too graphic to describe. In the middle of that dream, however, I began to quote the third chapter of Colossians my family and I committed to memory that week:

> If then you have been raised up with Christ, keep seeking the things above, where Christ is, seated at the right hand of God. Set your mind on the things above, not on the things that are on earth. For you have died and your life is hidden with Christ in God. When Christ, who is our life, is revealed, then you also will be revealed with Him in glory.

Without pause, my dream continued from the fifth verse:

> Therefore consider the members of your earthly body as dead to immorality, impurity, passion, evil desire, and greed, which amounts to idolatry. For it is on account of these things that the wrath of God will come, and in them you also once walked, when you were living in them. But now you also, put them all aside: anger, wrath, malice, slander, and abusive speech from your mouth. Do not lie to one another, since you laid aside the old self with its evil practices, and have put on the new self who s being renewed to a true knowledge according to the image of the One who created him — a renewal in which there is no distinction between Greek and Jew, circumcised and uncircumcised, barbarian, Scythian, slave and freeman, but Christ is all, and in all.

I wasn't done. It was almost as if I was driving a stake in the heart of the evil thoughts as I continued on from the twelfth verse:

> And so, as those who have been chosen of God, holy and beloved, put on a heart of compassion, kindness, humility, gentleness and patience; bearing with one another, and forgiving each other, whoever has a complaint against any one; just as *the Lord*

the Lord forgave you, so also should you. And beyond all these things put on love, which is the perfect bond of unity. And let the peace of Christ rule in your hearts, to which indeed you were called in one body; and be thankful. Let the word of Christ richly dwell within you, with all wisdom teaching and admonishing one another with psalms and hymns and spiritual songs, singing with thankfulness in your hearts to God.

To my amazement, I woke up reciting the seventeenth verse:

Whatever you do in word or deed, do all in the name of the Lord Jesus, giving thanks through Him to God the Father.

Instead of feeling defeated, as I often did when these dreams occurred, I arose from my bed claiming an amazing victory. I also learned a lesson I have never forgotten. God's Word truly can become deeply hidden in *the inner recesses of my heart*, exactly where I need it most. The promise of Psalm 119:9-11 had never been more real:

How can a young man keep his way pure?
By keeping it according to Your word.
With all my heart I have sought You;
Do not let me wander from Your commandments.
Your word I have treasured in my heart,
That I may not sin against You (Psalm 119:9-11).

(Adapted from "The Purity War: A Biblical Guide to Living in an Immoral World." By Dr. James M. Cecy)

3. Make the Presentation

Use the following sample message structure - obviously the shorter the presentation the less points.

SAMPLE MESSAGE STRUCTURE

Introduction to the Message

      Opening Illustration
      Presentation of the Background to the Text
      Reading of Text
      Presentation of Theme
      (Transition to First Main Point)

I. First Main Point

      Read the Text
      Explain the Text
      Share the Principle
      Illustrate the Point
      Apply the Truth
      (Transition to Second Main Point)

II. Second Main Point

      Read the Text
      Explain the Text
      Share the Principle
      Illustrate the Point
      Apply the Truth
      (Transition to Third Main Point)

III. Third Main Point

      Read the Text
      Explain the Text
      Share the Principle
      Illustrate the Point
      Apply the Truth
      (Transition to Conclusion)

Conclusion to the Message

      Review the Theme
      Challenge to Obey
      Closing Illustration

---

4. Scan or File All Research and Message Notes.

Don't even think of burying or throwing away those hard-earned study notes. Whether electronically scanned or physically filed, we must keep all our research, even the notes we do not use. Some folks file by topics; others by the specific biblical reference. The choice is ours as long as we are consistent and our system allows us to find our research easily.

Some of us have adopted the lifestyle that prides itself in desks piled high with paper. We abuse the intention of what King Solomon wrote, "Where no oxen are, the manger is clean . . . " (Proverbs 14:4). He is not making an excuse for clutter and disorder. Quite the contrary. An effective Bible student knows what he/she has studied and where to find it when needed.

For Further Study:

To listen to or download Dr. Cecy's messages and study outlines, visit the media section at www.campusbiblechurch.com

---

OUR PRIMARY FOCUS

It has been well said that the Bible is a HIM book. It's focus is none other than Him—the Lord Jesus Christ. Jesus Himself said,

> "You search the Scriptures because you think that in them you have eternal life; it is these that testify about Me" (Matthew 5:39; cf. Acts 8:30-31, 35).

I love the story about a great orator who traveled around the country reciting poetry and other great works. In one particular place he was asked to recite the 23rd Psalm—which he had done hundreds of times before. He stood and recited: "The Lord is my shepherd, I shall not want . . . " The people were astonished at the clarity and beauty in which he spoke those words. When he had finished the last verse of the well- known psalm the people stood and applauded for minutes.

There in the audience was an old missionary who had just returned from decades of overseas ministry. He stood before the audience and they fell silent. He, too, began to recite the 23rd Psalm. Though his voice was feeble and hoarse, there wasn't a dry eye in the house.

The old missionary sat down and the famous orator stood, wiping the tears from his own eyes. He looked at the crowd and said very humbly, "I know the 23rd Psalm. It's obvious to me, this man knows the Shepherd!"

It is my prayer that throughout this season of discovering the wonders of becoming effective Bible students we will not miss hearing the Shepherd's voice as we have never heard it before. May we all come to know Him in a new and even more personal way!

"I am the good shepherd, and I know My own and My own know Me . . . " (John 10:14).

"My sheep hear My voice and I know them, and they follow Me and I give eternal life to them, and they will never perish; and no one will snatch them out of the Father's hand" (John 10:27-28).

APPENDIX

ADDITIONAL
HELPS FOR
EFFECTIVE
BIBLE STUDY

APPENDIX 1
A POCKET GUIDE FOR EFFECTIVE BIBLE STUDY

The following is a brief overview of the five-step process. Make a copy and place this in your Bible.

Step One: Preparation - Anticipating God's Direction

1. Begin with prayer (Praising, Repenting, Asking, Yielding, Entreating, Rejoicing).
2. Make a commitment to strive to find the single meaning of the text.
3. Proceed with caution—drawing conclusions from the facts of Scripture (inductive exegesis).

Step Two: Observation - Asking The Right Questions

1. Study the background of the book (See Appendix 2 and do a survey on the book and Appendix 3 and do a character study of the author).
2. Read the entire book and chapter a number of times in many translations.
3. Examine carefully the specific passage in many translations.
4. Ask appropriate questions (Who? What? Where? When? How? Why?).
5. Look up cross-references.
6. Write down any further observations.

Step Three: Interpretation - Answering The Right Questions

1. Do particular word studies (synonyms, antonyms, figures of speech, idioms, repeated words and phrases, etc.).
2. Watch for specific details in the grammar (tenses, voices, moods, person, number, prepositions, conjunctions, etc.).
3. Write down what others say about the text.
4. Begin problem solving—deciding on what seems to be the best view.

Step Four: Application - Applying The Right Answers

1. Answer the question: So what?

2. List commands to obey, promises to keep, truths to know, actions to take, sins to forsake, examples to follow, things to avoid, new thoughts about God (Father, Son and Holy Spirit).

Step Five: Presentation - Announcing The Good News

1. Organize the presentation.

2. Select appropriate illustrations.

3. Make the presentation (Intro, Main Points, Conclusion).

4. Scan or file all research and message notes.

APPENDIX 2
HOW TO DO A SURVEY OF A BOOK OF THE BIBLE

Using the Bible and any other resources available, complete this form on each Bible book. Make sure you write down any pertinent Scripture references. File these surveys.

1. What is the name of the book and its meaning? _____

2. In which testament is it found? _____

3. Who was the author? _____

4. Who was he and why might he have been chosen by God to write this book? _____

5. In what language did he write this book? _____

6. To whom did he write? _____

7. What is the approximate time of the writing? _____

8. What are the main historical events surrounding the writing of this book? _____

9. Does this book conform to a book in the other testament? _____

10. What is the main subject? _____

11. What is the key verse(s)? _____
    _____

12. What are the main divisions? _____
    _____

13. What was the author's main purpose for writing? _____

_____

14. What was his special emphasis? _____

_____

15. What are the repeated phrases? _____

_____

16. What special names for God, Christ or the Holy Spirit does he

use? _____

_____

17. List the special chapters or portions: _____

_____

_____

18. Who are the main characters of the book? _____

_____

19. Are there any prominent doctrines emphasized? _____

_____

20. How does this book speak of the Lord? _____

_____

21. Anything else that is outstanding or different? _____

_____

22. What is especially precious in this book? _____

_____

23. My brief summary of the book is as follows: _____

_____

_____

_____

_____

_____

_____

_____

_____

_____

_____

_____

_____

APPENDIX 3
HOW TO DO A BIBLICAL CHARACTER STUDY

Using the Bible and any other resources available, attempt to complete this form on each biblical character. Make sure you write down any pertinent Scripture references. File these character studies.

1. What is his/her name?_____

2. What is the basic meaning of the name?_____

3. Was the name changed? To what?_____

   _____

4. What is the meaning of his/her new name?_____

5. Are there any other names for this character? _____

6. What was his/her date of birth and closest key historical event?

   _____

7. Was there divine intervention in the circumstances of his/her birth?

   Explain:_____

   _____

8. What are his/her parents' names?_____

9. Are there any further details concerning his/her parents?_____

   _____

10. What were his/her grandparents' names?_____

    _____

11. Are there any significant details concerning grandparents? _____

_____

12. Who are his/her brothers or sisters? _____

_____

13. What are the details concerning his/here brothers or sisters?

_____

14. What was the religious atmosphere in his/her home? _____

_____

15. What was the social status of the family? _____

_____

16. Were there any important childhood events? _____

_____

17. What was his/her spouse's name? _____

18. What were his/her children's names? _____

_____

19. What are the key points concerning his/her attitudes and emotions?

_____

20. What were his/her significant relationship (friends, enemies, etc.)?

_____

21. What was his/her relationship to God like? _____

_____

22. What was his/her conversion experience?_____

_____

23. What were his/her major spiritual victories?_____

_____

24. What were his/her major spiritual failures?_____

_____

25. What was the progression of his/her spiritual life?_____

_____

26. What were the circumstances surrounding his/her death? _____

_____

27. In what context is he/she mentioned in the other testament? In other

    books of the Bible? _____

_____

28. What primary lessons do we learn from his/her life?_____

_____

_____

_____

"Now these things happened as examples for us, that we should not crave evil things, as they also craved. And do not be idolaters, as some of them were . . . Nor let us act immorally, as some of them did . . . Nor let us try the Lord, as some of them did . . . Nor grumble as some of them did . . . Now these things happened to them as an example, and they were written for our instruction . . . Therefore let him who thinks he stands take heed lest he fall" (1 Corinthians 10:6-12).

APPENDIX 4
INSTRUCTIONS FOR INTERPRETING PARABLES

A parable is a short, fictitious narrative about some human experience well known to the hearer and designed to teach a spiritual lesson. It has been said that a parable is "an earthly story with a heavenly meaning."

The parables of Jesus occur only in the synoptic gospels (Matthew, Mark and Luke) with Luke's gospel containing the most. Scholars are not in agreement as to the exact number of parables but estimates are between 28 and 40.

In fulfillment of Old Testament prophecy (cf. Isaiah 6:9-10), Jesus taught using parables in order to unfold some Kingdom Principle to genuine truth-seekers while at the same time hiding these precious truths from those who were not sincere truth-seekers (Read Mark 4:11-12). It is therefore imperative that we learn how to interpret these important portions of Scripture carefully.

Using our Bible and any other available resources, try to answer the following questions to determine the meaning of the parable. Begin by reading the parable over at least three times (preferably in three different translations) before attempting to answer these questions:

1. Name the parable and passage(s) where it is located:._____

_____

2. Where is Christ and to whom is He speaking? _____

_____

3. From what segment of first-century society are the details of the parable? (e.g. farming, ruling class, economics, business, slaves, family, fishing, etc.) _____

_____

4. Are there unbelievers present? _____

5. Which of the gospel writers records this parable? _____

_____

6. Why is this significant in light of the theme of that gospel? (Note: Matthew presents Christ as King; Mark presents Him as Servant; Luke presents Him as Man and John presents Him as God).

_____

_____

7. Does Christ give the parable as a result of a direct question? _____

_____

8. Suggest a question that would be answered by the parable if none is given in the context: _____

_____

9. Does the parable answer a criticism made? _____

_____

10. Does Christ or the context interpret the parable? Explain.

_____

11. What is the main point (i.e. the Kingdom Principle) Christ is illustrating? (Note: Be careful not to over interpret every detail of a parable. Certain details are just a part of the parabolic imagery and have no specific meaning.) _____

_____

_____

_____

_____

12. What doctrine does the parable illustrate? (Note: Parables are generally not to be treated as primary sources of doctrine but as supporting passages for doctrines already clearly revealed elsewhere in Scripture.)

_____

_____

_____

13. Can you give any cross-reference, especially from the epistles, that clearly state the doctrine taught in this parable?

_____

_____

14. What significance, if any, does this parable have for us today? Do the same principles and doctrines apply?

_____

_____

15. What do other commentaries and resources say about this parable?

_____

_____

_____

_____

_____

_____

_____

_____

16. Give a summary of the parable and its meaning. _____

_____

_____

_____

_____

_____

_____

_____

_____

_____

_____

_____

_____

_____

_____

_____

_____

_____

_____

_____

APPENDIX 5
"GOD HAS SPOKEN IN HIS MARVELOUS WORD"

An Outline of Psalm 19:7-14

Psalm 19:7-14

The law of the Lord is perfect, restoring the soul;
The testimony of the Lord is sure, making wise the simple.
The precepts of the Lord are right, rejoicing the heart;
The commandment of the Lord is pure, enlightening the eyes.
The fear of the Lord is clean, enduring forever;
The judgments of the Lord are true; they are righteous altogether.
They are more desirable than gold, yes, than much fine gold;
Sweeter also than honey and the drippings of the honeycomb.
Moreover, by them Your servant is warned;
In keeping them there is great reward.
Who can discern his errors? Acquit me of hidden faults.
Also keep back Your servant from presumptuous sins;
Let them not rule over me;
Then I will be blameless,
And I shall be acquitted of great transgression.
Let the words of my mouth and the meditation of my heart
Be acceptable in Your sight,
O Lord, my rock and my Redeemer.

I. David's Detailed Description of the Word of God (Psalm 19:7-9)

A. Six Facets of the Word of God

Facet #1. The Word of God presents us with the LAW of the Lord.

Facet #2. The Word of God presents us with TESTIMONY of the Lord.

Facet #3. The Word of God presents us with the PRECEPTS of the Lord.

Facet #4. The Word of God presents us with the COMMANDS of the Lord.

Facet #5. The Word of God presents us with the FEAR the Lord.

Facet #6. The Word of God presents us with the JUDGMENTS of the Lord.

B. Six Characteristics of the Word of God

1. The Word of God is PERFECT.

2. The Word of God is SURE.

3. The Word of God is RIGHT.

4. The Word of God is PURE.

5. The Word of God is CLEAN.

6. The Word of God is TRUE.

- 2 Timothy 3:16-17 "All Scripture is inspired by God (i.e. God-breathed) and profitable for teaching, for reproof, for correction, for training in righteousness; so that the man of God may be adequate, equipped for every good work."

- Hebrews 4:12 "For the word of God is living and active and sharper than any two-edged sword, and piercing as far as the division of soul and spirit, of both joints and marrow, and able to judge the thoughts and intentions of the heart."

C. Six Ways the Word of God Impacts Our Lives

1. The Word of God RESTORES THE SOUL.

2. The Word of God MAKES WISE THE SIMPLE.

3. The Word of God REJOICES THE HEART.

4. The Word of God ENLIGHTENS THE EYES.

5. The Word of God ENDURES FOREVER.

6. The Word of God IS ALTOGETHER RIGHTEOUS.

II. David's Deep-Seated Attraction to the Word of God (Psalm 19:10-11)

Testimony #1 "The Word of God is more desirable to me than riches."

- Psalm 19:10 "They are more desirable than gold, yes, than much fine gold . . . "
- Psalm 119:14 "I have rejoiced in the way of Your testimonies, as much as in all riches."
- Psalm 119:72 "The law of Your mouth is better to me than thousands of gold and silver pieces."
- Psalm 119:127 "Therefore I love Your commandments above gold, yes, above fine gold."

Testimony #2. "The Bible is sweeter than the sweetest thing in my life."

- Psalm 19:10 " . . . sweeter also than honey and the drippings of the honeycomb."
- Psalm 119:103 "How sweet are Your words to my taste! Yes, sweeter than honey to my mouth!"

Testimony #3. "The Word of God is the source of valuable protection in my life."

- Psalm 19:11 "Moreover, by them Your servant is warned . . . "
- Psalm 119:9-11 "How can a young man keep his way pure? By keeping it according to Your word. With all my heart I have sought You; do not let me wander from Your commandments. Your word I have treasured in my heart, that I may not sin against You."

Testimony #4. "The Word of God is the source of great reward in my life."

- Psalm 19:11 " . . . in keeping them there is great reward."

- Joshua 1:8 "This book of the law shall not depart from your mouth, but you shall meditate on it day and night, so that you may be careful to do according to all that is written in it; for then you will make your way prosperous, and then you will have success."

- Psalm 1:2-3 "But his delight is in the law of the LORD, and in His law he meditates day and night. He will be like a tree firmly planted by streams of water, which yields its fruit in its season and its leaf does not wither; and in whatever he does, he prospers."

III. David's Desperate Conviction Regarding the Word of God (Psalm 19:12-13)

- Psalm 19:12-13 "Who can discern his errors? Acquit me of hidden faults. Also keep back Your servant from presumptuous sins; let them not rule over me; then I will be blameless, and I shall be acquitted of great transgression."

- Hebrews 4:13 "And there is no creature hidden from His sight, but all things are open and laid bare to the eyes of Him with whom we have to do."

- Psalm 51:1-2 "Be gracious to me, O God, according to Your lovingkindness; according to the greatness of Your compassion blot out my transgressions. Wash me thoroughly from my iniquity and cleanse me from my sin."

- Psalm 139:23-24 "Search me, O God, and know my heart; try me and know my anxious thoughts; and see if there be any hurtful way in me and lead me in the everlasting way."

IV. David's Daily Devotion to the God of the Bible (Psalm 19:14)

- Psalm 19:14 "Let the words of my mouth and the meditation of my heart be acceptable in Your sight, O Lord, my rock and my Redeemer."

The Challenge:

The road to becoming a man or woman of the Word begins with a journey of the heart!

- 1 Corinthians 1:14-16 "But a natural man does not accept the things of the Spirit of God, for they are foolishness to him; and he cannot understand them, because they are spiritually appraised. But he who is spiritual appraises all things, yet he himself is appraised by no one. For WHO HAS KNOWN THE MIND OF THE LORD, THAT HE WILL INSTRUCT HIM? But we have the mind of Christ."

- Psalm 19:14 "Let the words of my mouth and the meditation of my heart be acceptable in Your sight, O Lord, my rock and my Redeemer. "

- Ecclesiastes 12:11-14 "The words of wise men are like goads, and masters of these collections are like well-driven nails; they are given by one Shepherd. But beyond this, my son, be warned: the writing of many books is endless, and excessive devotion to books is wearying to the body. The conclusion, when all has been heard, is: fear God and keep His commandments, because this applies to every person. For God will bring every act to judgment, everything which is hidden, whether it is good or evil."

- 2 Timothy 2:15 "Be diligent to present yourself approved to God as a workman who does not need to be ashamed, handling accurately the word of truth"

APPENDIX 6
BIBLE READING RECORD

Books	Chapters
Genesis	1 2 3 4 5 6 7 8 9 10 11 12 13 14 15 16 17 18 19 20 21 22 23 24 25 26 27 28 29 30 31 32 33 34 35 36 37 38 39 40 41 42 43 44 45 46 47 48 49 50
Exodus	1 2 3 4 5 6 7 8 9 10 11 12 13 14 15 16 17 18 19 20 21 22 23 24 25 26 27 28 29 30 31 32 33 34 35 36 37 38 39 40
Leviticus	1 2 3 4 5 6 7 8 9 10 11 12 13 14 15 16 17 18 19 20 21 22 23 24 25 26 27
Numbers	1 2 3 4 5 6 7 8 9 10 11 12 13 14 15 16 17 18 19 20 21 22 23 24 25 26 27 28 29 30 31 32 33 34 35 36
Deuteronomy	1 2 3 4 5 6 7 8 9 10 11 12 13 14 15 16 17 18 19 20 21 22 23 24 25 26 27 28 29 30 31 32 33 34
Joshua	1 2 3 4 5 6 7 8 9 10 11 12 13 14 15 16 17 18 19 20 21 22 23 24
Judges	1 2 3 4 5 6 7 8 9 10 11 12 13 14 15 16 17 18 19 20 21
Ruth	1 2 3 4
1 Samuel	1 2 3 4 5 6 7 8 9 10 11 12 13 14 15 16 17 18 19 20 21 22 23 24 25 26 27 28 29 30 31
2 Samuel	1 2 3 4 5 6 7 8 9 10 11 12 13 14 15 16 17 18 19 20 21 22 23 24
1 Kings	1 2 3 4 5 6 7 8 9 10 11 12 13 14 15 16 17 18 19 20 21 22
2 Kings	1 2 3 4 5 6 7 8 9 10 11 12 13 14 15 16 17 18 19 20 21 22 23 24 25

1 Chronicles	1 2 3 4 5 6 7 8 9 10 11 12 13 14 15 16 17 18 19 20 21 22 23 24 25 26 27 28 29
2 Chronicles	1 2 3 4 5 6 7 8 9 10 11 12 13 14 15 16 17 18 19 20 21 22 23 24 25 26 27 28 29 30 31 32 33 34 35 36
Ezra	1 2 3 4 5 6 7 8 9 10
Nehemiah	1 2 3 4 5 6 7 8 9 10 11 12 13
Esther	1 2 3 4 5 6 7 8 9 10
Job	1 2 3 4 5 6 7 8 9 10 11 12 13 14 15 16 17 18 19 20 21 22 23 24 25 26 27 28 29 30 31 32 33 34 35 36 37 38 39 40 41 42
Psalms	1 2 3 4 5 6 7 8 9 10 11 12 13 14 15 16 17 18 19 20 21 22 23 24 25 26 27 28 29 30 31 32 33 34 35 36 37 38 39 40 41 42 43 44 45 46 47 48 49 50 51 52 53 54 55 56 57 58 59 60 61 62 63 64 65 66 67 68 69 70 71 72 73 74 75 76 77 78 79 80 81 82 83 84 85 86 87 88 89 90 91 92 93 94 95 96 97 98 99 100 101 102 103 104 105 106 107 108 109 110 111 112 113 114 115 116 117 118 119 120 121 122 123 124 125 126 127 128 129 130 131 132 133 134 135 136 137 138 139 140 141 142 143 144 145 146 147 148 149 150
Proverbs	1 2 3 4 5 6 7 8 9 10 11 12 13 14 15 16 17 18 19 20 21 22 23 24 25 26 27 28 29 30 31
Ecclesiastes	1 2 3 4 5 6 7 8 9 10 11 12
Song of Solomon	1 2 3 4 5 6 7 8
Isaiah	1 2 3 4 5 6 7 8 9 10 11 12 13 14 15 16 17 18 19 20 21 22 23 24 25 26 27 28 29 30 31 32 33 34 35 36 37 38 39 40 41 42 43 44 45 46 47 48 49 50 51 52 53 54 55 56 57 58 59 60 61 62 63 64 65 66

Jeremiah	1 2 3 4 5 6 7 8 9 10 11 12 13 14 15 16 17 18 19 20 21 22 23 24 25 26 27 28 29 30 31 32 33 34 35 36 37 38 39 40 41 42 43 44 45 46 47 48 49 50 51 52
Lamentations	1 2 3 4 5
Ezekiel	1 2 3 4 5 6 7 8 9 10 11 12 13 14 15 16 17 18 19 20 21 22 23 24 25 26 27 28 29 30 31 32 33 34 35 36 37 38 39 40 41 42 43 44 45 46 47 48
Daniel	1 2 3 4 5 6 7 8 9 10 11 12
Hosea	1 2 3 4 5 6 7 8 9 10 11 12 13 14
Joel	1 2 3
Amos	1 2 3 4 5 6 7 8 9
Obadiah	1
Jonah	1 2 3 4
Micah	1 2 3 4 5 6 7
Nahum	1 2 3
Habakkuk	1 2 3
Zephaniah	1 2 3
Haggai	1 2
Zechariah	1 2 3 4 5 6 7 8 9 10 11 12 13 14
Malachi	1 2 3 4

Matthew	1 2 3 4 5 6 7 8 9 10 11 12 13 14 15 16 17 18 19 20 21 22 23 24 25 26 27 28
Mark	1 2 3 4 5 6 7 8 9 10 11 12 13 14 15 16
Luke	1 2 3 4 5 6 7 8 9 10 11 12 13 14 15 16 17 18 19 20 21 22 23 24
John	1 2 3 4 5 6 7 8 9 10 11 12 13 14 15 16 17 18 19 20 21
Acts	1 2 3 4 5 6 7 8 9 10 11 12 13 14 15 16 17 18 19 20 21 22 23 24 25 26 27 28
Romans	1 2 3 4 5 6 7 8 9 10 11 12 13 14 15 16
1 Corinthians	1 2 3 4 5 6 7 8 9 10 11 12 13 14 15 16
2 Corinthians	1 2 3 4 5 6 7 8 9 10 11 12 13
Galatians	1 2 3 4 5 6
Ephesians	1 2 3 4 5 6
Philippians	1 2 3 4
Colossians	1 2 3 4
1 Thessalonians	1 2 3 4 5
2 Thessalonians	1 2 3
1 Timothy	1 2 3 4 5 6
2 Timothy	1 2 3 4
Titus	1 2 3
Philemon	1
Hebrews	1 2 3 4 5 6 7 8 9 10 11 12 13
James	1 2 3 4 5

1 Peter	1 2 3 4 5
2 Peter	1 2 3
1 John	1 2 3 4 5
2 John	1
3 John	1
Jude	1
Revelation	1 2 3 4 5 6 7 8 9 10 11 12 13 14 15 16 17 18 19 20 21 22

"So great is my veneration for the Bible that the earlier my children begin to read, the more confident will be my hope that they will prove useful citizens of their country and respectable members of society. I have for many years made it a practice to read through the Bible once every year."
(John Quincy Adams)

"I have read the Bible through one hundred times, and always with increasing delight."
(George Muller)

APPENDIX 7
BIBLE DIVISIONS

Old Testament (39)

Pentateuch (Torah) (5)

- Genesis
- Exodus
- Leviticus
- Numbers
- Deuteronomy

Israel's History (12)

- Joshua
- Judges
- Ruth
- 1 Samuel
- 2 Samuel
- 1 Kings
- 2 Kings
- 1 Chronicles
- 2 Chronicles
- Ezra
- Nehemiah
- Esther

Poetry & Wisdom (5)

- Job
- Psalm
- Proverbs
- Ecclesiastes
- Song of Solomon

The Prophets (17)

Major (5)

- Isaiah
- Jeremiah
- Lamentations
- Ezekiel
- Daniel

Minor* (12)

- Hosea
- Joel
- Amos
- Obadiah
- Jonah
- Micah
- Nahum
- Habakkuk
- Zephaniah
- Haggai
- Zechariah
- Malachi

* Minor because of size not importance

New Testament (27)

Gospels (4)

- Matthew
- Mark
- Luke
- John

Historical (1)

- Acts

Epistles (Letters) (21)

- Romans
- 1 Corinthians
- 2 Corinthians
- Galatians
- Ephesians
- Philippians
- Colossians
- 1 Thessalonians
- 2 Thessalonians
- 1 Timothy
- 2 Timothy
- Titus
- Philemon
- Hebrews
- James
- 1 Peter
- 2 Peter
- 1 John
- 2 John
- 3 John
- Jude

Prophetic (1)

- Revelation

APPENDIX 8
JUST FOR FUN

I hope you are familiar with the names of all 66 books of the Bible. If not, take a moment to turn to the index of your Bible (or Appendix 6 of the workbook) and complete the following exercise. One book is underlined to help you start. Can you find the other 14? (The answers are at the bottom of the page.)

> In these remarks are hidden the names of 15 books of the Bible. It's a real lulu. Kept me looking so hard for facts I missed the <u>revelation</u>. I was in a real jam especially since the names were not capitalized. The truth will come to numbers of our readers. To others, it will be a real job. For all it will be a most fascinating search. Yes, there will be some easy to spot, others hard to judge. So we admit it usually results in loud lamentations when we can't find them. One lady says she brews coffee while she puzzles over it.

Answers: Mark, Luke, Kings, Acts, Revelation, James, Ruth, Numbers, Job, Amos, Esther, Judges, Titus, Lamentations, Hebrews

72

APPENDIX 9
HOW TO USE THIS SELF-STUDY WORKBOOK IN GROUP STUDY

Session #1 — INTRODUCTION

Date of Class: _____

Reading due: Pages 7-14 and Appendix 5

Session #2 — PART ONE: Doctrinal Presuppositions

Date of Class: _____

Reading due: Pages 15-20

If applicable, complete all assignments in this section.

In-Class Assignment:

Each participant will come prepared to share a Bible text of no more than 2-3 verses to work through during this course. (The group may decide to work together on the same passage.)

Session #3 — PART TWO: Divine Prerequisites

PART THREE: Doctrinal Publications

Date of Class: _____

Reading due: Pages 21-31

If applicable, complete all assignments in this section.

In-Class Assignment:

Each participant will come with a completed personal testimony (Page 22) and a list of their personal Bible study tools (Using the list on page 29-32). Specific instructions will be given by the instructor or fellow classmates on the use of some of the available Bible Study tools.

Session #4 — PART FOUR: Designated Principles (Continued)

Step One: Preparation

Step Two: Observation

Date of Class: _____

Reading due: Page 32-36

> If applicable complete all assignments in this section.

In-Class Assignment:

> Using the instructions, each participant will come prepared with a page of observations of their assigned text.

Session #5 — PART FOUR: Designated Principles (Continued)

Step Three: Interpretation

Step Four: Application

Date of Class: _____

Reading due: Pages 37-40

In-Class Assignment:

> Each participant will come prepared to submit their research and application of their text. Time will also be given in class to work on the final research.

Session #6 — PART FOUR: Designated Principles: (Continued)

Step Five: Presentation

Date of Class: _____

Reading due: Pages 41-46

In-Class Assignment:

> Each participant will come prepared to present in writing and/or make a final presentation of his/her Bible message. Length of time to be determined.

OPTIONAL FOR EIGHT SESSION STUDY:

You may want to insert the following between Session #5 and Session #6

Option Session A   How to Do a Survey of the Bible

How to Do a Biblical Character Study

Date of Class: _____

Reading Due: Appendix 2-3

In-Class Assignment:

>Each participant will submit a completed survey of a Bible book (using Appendix 2) and will also turn in a copy of a completed biblical character study (using Appendix 3)

Option Session B   Instructions for Interpreting Parables

Date of Class: _____

Reading due: Appendix 4

In-Class Assignment:

>Each participant will come prepared with a completed parable (using Appendix 4)

APPENDIX 10
SCRIPTURE INDEX

SCRIPTURE INDEX

(Continued)

STANDING ON THE PROMISES

R. Kelso Carter (1849-1926)

Verse 1

Standing on the promises of Christ my King,
Through eternal ages let his praises ring;
Glory in the highest, I will shout and sing,
Standing on the promises of God.

Refrain:

Standing, standing,
Standing on the promises of Christ my Savior;
Standing, standing,
I'm standing on the promises of God.

Verse 2

Standing on the promises that cannot fail,
When the howling storms of doubt and fear assail,
By the living Word of God I shall prevail,
Standing on the promises of God.

[Refrain]

Verse 3

Standing on the promises of Christ the Lord,
Bound to him eternally by love's strong cord,
Overcoming daily with the Spirit's sword,
Standing on the promises of God.

[Refrain]

Verse 4

Standing on the promises I cannot fall,
listening every moment to the Spirit's call,
resting in my Savior as my all in all,
standing on the promises of God.

[Refrain]

OPEN MY EYES

Clara H. Scott (1841-1897)

Verse 1
  Open my eyes, that I may see
  Glimpses of truth Thou hast for me;
  Place in my hands the wonderful key
  That shall unclasp and set me free.

Refrain:
  Silently now I wait for Thee,
  Ready my God, Thy will to see,
  Open my eyes, illumine me,
  Spirit divine!

Verse 2
  Open my ears, that I may hear
  Voices of truth Thou sendest clear;
  And while the wave notes fall on my ear,
  Everything false will disappear.

[Refrain]

Verse 3
  Open my mouth, and let me bear,
  Gladly the warm truth everywhere;
  Open my heart and let me prepare
  Love with Thy children thus to share.

[Refrain]

OTHER MATERIALS BY

DR. JIM CECY

Available Though

JARON MINISTRIES

INTERNATIONAL, INC.

www.jaron.org

www.puritywar.com

www.ingramcontent.com/pod-product-compliance
Lightning Source LLC
Chambersburg PA
CBHW071019040426
42443CB00007B/857